Me, My Dad and the New York Mets

by Valerie Pepe

New Paltz, New York

© Copyright 2025 by Valerie Pepe

All rights reserved. No part of this book may be reproduced, scanned, or distributed in any printed, or electronic form, including recording, photocopying, taping or by any information storage retrieval system now known or to be invented without the permission of the author except in the case of brief quotations embodied in critical articles and reviews in a magazine, newspaper or broadcast. Please do not participate in or encourage piracy of copyrighted materials in violation of the author's rights. Purchase only authorized editions.

ISBN: 979-8-9991491-0-7
Cover design by Olivia Hansen
Published by MediacsBooks@gmail.com
Also available as an eBook.

A friend once said to me, "You are writing another book? How much can you write about yourself?" I smiled because this memoir is not just about me. It's about the relationship between a father, a daughter, and their shared love of baseball.

Preface

This book is dedicated to my father, Eugene Pepe, a diehard baseball fan, player and lifelong teacher of the game who grew up playing baseball on the streets of Manhattan's Lower East Side. His words gifted me, his physically disabled daughter, with an understanding of the sport and a deep appreciation of how the love of baseball can bring together those you love.

To all those who say baseball is too slow and often boring, I say you're not having the experience. There are very few things in life that are more exciting than watching a first baseman make an impossible catch to save a run from scoring, or a batter hit a walk-off home run to win a game.

Dad mowing the lawn at my Great-Grandmother Saracino's house in Trenton, New Jersey

Meet Dad. Or is He Tony Bennett?

My dad was a slender man who maintained a weight of 160 to 172 pounds. He had the Italian 'olive' completion, and often passed for a Puerto Rican. He stood 5-feet 11-inches tall. When he was younger, his hair was black and thick. As he got older, he started to bald.

When I was 8 or 9, Dad would go to the local barber shop that charged only $8.00 for a cut. I never understood what hair he was getting cut because he had very little. His hair was receding on both sides and balding at the top. But he never went completely bald and took pride in his appearance his whole life.

In old photos of him and my parents' wedding photos, he has thick hair. I don't know if he missed it or not. Maybe when he gave the barber instructions, he imagined he still had thick hair. When he got dressed for a party or a wedding, he would carefully slick what he had left of his hair. He must have used a "product" because his hair was so shiny. I thought if I touched it, the hair would slide off onto my fingers.

I'm not sure where Dad got his sense of color coordination—maybe in the Marines. But he had it. His socks always matched the color of the suit or jacket he was wearing. He always dressed appropriately for any occasion. His dress code was strict, appropriate for every occasion, almost military in its correctness and discipline. He had a lot of self-pride, which I also have. I love clothes and dress well every day, just like my dad.

In one old photo, Dad is wearing a plaid blazer with beige patches on the elbows. Elbow patches were very popular in the 1970s.

Dad always felt great when someone said he didn't look his age, even when he got old and infirm. "Emma," he'd ask my mom, "did you hear the nurse thought I was only 60 years old?"

Mom would reply, "Oh really, she said that?" Then she would turn to me and wink, and I would bite my lip and try not not to laugh.

After my Dad died in 2019, life was never the same for me or my mom. My parents had been married for 61 years at the time of his death. He was always there for both of us. And now, suddenly, he wasn't.

Mom and Dad

Dad died on October 28, 2019, the 33rd anniversary of the New York Mets' World Series Parade up the Canyon of Heroes. The date seemed fitting for one of the greatest Mets' fans in history. Other than my mom, Dad was passionate about the Mets. The team was a special part of his life— not just the players and the managers, but the game of baseball itself.

That's how I will always remember him in my heart.

Dad was a big New York Giants baseball fan. He told me Willie Mays was the greatest player he had ever seen play the game. When the Giants moved to San Francisco in 1958, many diehard fans felt betrayed. Dad didn't feel that way and never stopped loving baseball. In 1962, when New York had a brand-new team to cheer for, my dad became an instant fan.

✳✳✳

I was born with Arthrogryposis Multiplex Congenita (AMC). My hips were so stiff and frozen, I couldn't walk without crutches. Unlike my brothers, Dad couldn't teach me how to play baseball. But that didn't stop him from sharing his knowledge of the game with me, his youngest child, his little girl. He taught me everything I know about baseball, about how professional players must be very disciplined—practice every day, eat healthy, develop their skills and love the sport passionately.

When baseball's spring training started in 2020, six months after Dad died, I had an empty feeling in my heart while watching a Sunday afternoon Mets game on Channel 11. Not only was Dad gone, but the stadiums were empty because of the COVID-19 pandemic. So to make myself feel a little better, I did what I did every Sunday when I watched the game with Dad: I dressed in my good luck Mets sweatshirt, sat on the living room rug, and had my snacks on the coffee table. Of course, just like Dad, I did not move if the Mets were leading. Dad was superstitious about the game. I am even worse. Often I cross my fingers and legs to help my team win the game.

✳✳✳

So, for those readers who wonder why I decided to write a baseball memoir, this is the reason: I loved my father, and I loved our baseball connection, which I still feel deeply to this day, almost six years after my Dad passed.

So let's pretend it's Sunday afternoon and the Mets game is on television. Sit back with me and my Dad and watch the game with us. Maybe you too will feel that special connection between a father who loved watching baseball with his daughter. I hope so!

Every Sunday

Sundays were not just for going to church. Sundays were also the day for the extended Pepe family to gather, consume great home-cooked food, and watch baseball. I think even God would agree that family, food, baseball and religion are equally important.

On Sunday mornings my house was filled with all sorts of activity and very LOUD sounds. The sound level in Italian American families is by tradition very high. If a stranger walked by our house, he would have thought we were fighting or arguing. We were not. We were just being ourselves.

Mom's kitchen on Sundays was an active restaurant that filled our house with the scent of homemade gravy and fresh baked

Dad and Mom at home celebrating his 80th birthday

bread. These scents were the natural alarm clock that woke me and my brothers up at 6:00 a.m. While most people would still be sleeping at that time, my grandmother and mother would be having a joint conference in the kitchen on the preparation of the Sunday meal.

While this conference took place, my brothers would come into my bedroom and reenact the World Wrestling Entertainment (WWE) on my bed with my stuffed animals. They would wrestle my dolls and body slam them on the mattress. Often, the dolls' limbs would go missing, which really upset me.

I was not a Raggedy Ann doll. I wore leg braces at night and my bed had metal guard rails to prevent me from falling onto the floor. But I loved my brothers' attention, and it was fun watching them wrestle with my dolls.

After my brothers, Eugene and Robert, got tired of wrestling with my dolls in my bedroom, we went to the living room and watched cartoons until Dad came in and turned off the TV. Dad sat in his brown recliner with the Sunday *Staten Island Advance* newspaper in hand, reading all the sections and giving us his critique on the politics of the day. At 11:00 a.m., he changed the channel to "The World at War" documentary series, and my brothers went back to their bedroom to read their comic books. I stayed in the living room with Dad.

Dad liked cartoons and the comic strips in the newspaper. Peanuts and Superman were his favorites. But as a former U.S. Marine who served during the time of the Korean War, he also had a serious side. During the war, he was stationed state-side in Norfolk, VA, and at Camp Pendleton in North Carolina. Dad was an expert typist, a subject he enjoyed in high school, and the Marines needed good typists on the home front. But there was always the possibility of him being transferred to a combat zone in Korea.

Dad was proud of his service and always believed he played an important role in the war effort.

So it wasn't surprising that he enjoyed watching serious programs like the weekly British documentary series, "The World at War." This 30-minute documentary was on from 11:00 to 11:30 a.m. every Sunday for 26 weeks in 1973. It showed highlights of World War II, using black and white archival footage. At the time, it was the most expensive documentary series ever made.

As a six-year-old, I really wanted to watch cartoons, but Dad had control of the television on Sundays. He worked five to six nights a week, so Sundays were his time to relax. I understood that.

But I wanted to be with him, so I hung out in the living room while he watched "The World at War," and played with my Barbie dolls. Occasionally, the narration caught my attention and I looked up at the screen. When Dad saw me watching the TV, he would explain to me what I was seeing. The images of suffering and death were strong and disturbing for an eight-year-old to process. But because my dad was there with me, and never hesitated to explain what I was seeing, I felt safe. I also felt a deepening appreciation of the sacrifices made by so many American soldiers like him.

My parents and grandparents wanted us kids to know history. I remember my dad telling me about the events leading up to World War II, the Holocaust, and the pro-Nazi rallies in Manhattan before the U.S. entered the war. History and the truth were a part of my family conversation starting when I was in elementary school.

Meanwhile, in the kitchen, Mom and Grandma Tessie were discussing what pasta and homemade gravy (what other Americans call "sauce") to cook for the day's main event —the family meal which always happened at 2 p.m. on Sundays.

We also watched comedies. When the Abbott and Costello movies aired at 11:30 a.m., right after the "The World at War," Dad's mood switched quickly from serious to fun-loving. He'd put down the newspaper, grab another cup of coffee, and call for Mom and my brothers to join us. Mom would come into the living room for a few minutes before returning to the kitchen. My brothers would show up and start fighting for the perfect place on the couch. The living room was filled with our laughter.

When the Abbott and Costello movie ended, "Kiner's Korner" started. This was the New York Mets pre-game show that featured interviews with players and coaches, and highlights of previous Mets games hosted by Mets broadcaster Ralph Kiner. Kiner was a home run hitter who played outfield for four different major league teams from 1946 to 1955. He was the

Met's TV announcer from 1962, when the team was founded, until his death in 2017.

My brother Eugene was a New York Yankee fan. So when the Mets game started, he retreated to his bedroom to listen to the Yankee game on his radio. On his way out of the living room, he would make a sarcastic comment like: "How often have the Mets been in the World Series?" We naturally ignored him and his snarky remarks about the Mets.

***

The Mets won their first World Series in 1969, when I was two. They won their second World Series in 1986, when I was 19. During that same period, from 1969 to 1986, the Yankees won two World Series.

Mom wasn't a diehard baseball fan. But living in a household of baseball fanatics, she became more interested in the sport as we kids got older. She became a big Mets fan, especially when they made it to the playoffs or World Series.

***

When "Kiner's Korner" ended, the game started. I wore my favorite Mets T-shirt to bring the team luck. And though we were in our living room at home, it felt as though we were at the stadium. Dad's excitement was intense, and so was mine. When the Mets made a great play or scored a run, he would jump up from his chair and cheer loudly.

We all knew when Grandma Tessie was setting the dining room table that Sunday dinner would be served soon. She always began with fresh fruit cups, prosciutto wrapped around thin bread sticks, and then the main course, a large bowl of ziti pasta soaked in her homemade gravy which she placed in the center of the table. Finally, she surrounded the large bowl of pasta with smaller bowls filled with a variety of vegetables, tossed salad and her homemade potato salad.

Eating at 2 p.m. on Sundays often interfered with our watching the Mets games on Channel 11, especially the home games that started at 1:30 p.m. But Dad was determined to find a way for us to keep following the game during the Sunday meal.

His first solution didn't work out too well. He put his transistor radio in his shirt pocket and tuned the radio to the game. I put my hand over my mouth to stop myself from giggling because I knew Dad was going to get into trouble. And, sure enough, when Mom and Grandma Tessie heard the voice of the Mets announcer, Bob Murphy, they gave a look to my Dad that prompted him to give me a wink and smile, and shut off the radio.

In our house, every meal was a sacred family occasion. If the telephone rang during dinner time, nobody answered it. Television and radio were forbidden. Nothing was more important than the family gathering together for a meal.

Dad soon found another way to listen to the game during the Sunday meal. He connected an earpiece to a long wire that ran from the transistor radio in his pants pocket. Nobody at the table seemed to notice this but me, and it made me giggle. Dad put his finger over this lips to tell me to be quiet. It was our secret. When Mom finally realized what was happening, she didn't say anything because all the children had already finished eating. She just shook her head.

I'm not sure if Grandma Tessie or Mom understood why watching the Mets on television on Sunday afternoons was so important to me and Dad. For Dad, it was the one day during the week he could relax and relive the baseball playing days of his youth. For me, it was an opportunity to be with a father I adored.

✶✶✶

I remember driving to Grandma Mary's house in Manhattan when I was eight years old. Sitting in the back seat of the car, I'm so short I can't see out of the windows. Mom is the driver in our family. Dad is the GPS. Mom doesn't like Dad telling her what to do or where to go. Her face is tightening with tension. She's relieved when we pass the baseball fields because she knows Dad will start talking about the homerun he hit to win a game, or the time he caught a ball in the outfield that sealed a win. Mom is now driver and GPS. Dad is reliving his childhood, adolescence, and his past glories on the baseball field. The tension in the car has dissipated.

Baseball and its Meaning

Today, many say that baseball is too slow and boring, that games take too long to play. In my opinion, those that say that are not true baseball fans. A baseball fan is passionate and loyal to their team. People who criticize the game need to learn the roots and meaning of baseball from those who play the game or love the game like I do. In my dreams, I sometimes wish I was born a boy and was good enough at baseball to make it to the major leagues.

For many Italian American teenagers like my father who grew up in the tenements and projects of the Lower East Side of Manhattan, the dream of becoming a professional baseball player was one way out of poverty. That was my Dad's dream. He dreamt of becoming the next Joe DiMaggio or Yogi Berra (both New York Yankees), or even a Ted Williams (Boston Red Sox). Unfortunately, that didn't happen.

Dad and his childhood friends spent every Saturday and Sunday afternoon playing baseball on the grassy fields that lined the Franklin Delanor Roosevelt Drive. They loved watching the game and they loved playing it. The FDR baseball fields were their *Field of Dreams*, just like the title of the movie with Kevin Costner and James Earl Jones.

Most of Dad's friends didn't have the money to buy gloves, bats and balls. But whatever they did have was shared without question. My dad was one of the few kids who owned a baseball glove which he shared with his best friend. He bought the glove with tips he got from his job delivering fresh chickens to homemakers in the tenements. The kids who didn't have gloves had to catch the hardball with their bare hands.

Back when my dad was a kid, scouts from major league teams came to the FDR baseball fields looking for talented players. My dad told me about the day a New York Yankee scout showed up. My dad had dislocated his right shoulder a few weeks before, and though he had mostly rehabilitated his injury with intensive exercises, he didn't do well at the plate.

But the thing about my dad was that while life could disappoint him, it never discouraged him. He was accepting. If he couldn't become a major league player, then he would use his knowledge and love of the sport to inspire his sons and the kids he coached as the manager of the Catholic Schools Little League Championship on Staten Island. Of course, he also passed on to me, his disabled daughter, a great passion for the sport.

The Spaulding baseball glove Dad bought when he was a kid

Playing Catch

It's a Sunday afternoon and we got the all-clear from Mom and Grandma that lunch is over, we've eaten enough, and we can go out and play. Kids are already outside playing softball and kickball. Car bumpers serve as bases, and the score is kept with chalk on the sidewalk. Everyone gets a chance to play, run and hit. Boys and girls are equal. But I can't play because I'm on crutches.

Dad heads for the basement and returns with a softball and his favorite baseball glove, the one he bought in the local sporting goods store when he was a kid. He throws the ball up in the air and catches it easily with his glove. He could have been a professional baseball player if he'd had the opportunity. I am sure of it.

"Anyone want to play catch out front?" he asks. He's talking to my older brothers, not to me, but I go out with them to watch. My brothers' baseball gloves are worn and marked up. I sit on the red brick steps and watch the three of them tossing the ball back and forth in the middle of Cooper Avenue. I'm wearing denim shorts and a pink T-shirt.

In other families, a girl like me with two brothers might be left out in a game of catch, even if she weren't on crutches. Not in my family. Not with a dad who is sensitive to my feelings.

"Let's have a time out," Dad tells my brothers. My brothers continue to throw the ball back and forth as Dad comes over to me. He is wearing a white undershirt, blue shorts, white socks up to his knees and the worn-out sneakers he bought on sale in Kmart. "I need you to help us," he says.

"Really?" I ask.

"I need you to be the lookout. When you see a car turning onto our street, I want you to scream out 'CAR!' Can you do that?"

"Yes, Daddy, I can!" Oh, I am so happy to be included, to be the "lookout." But I have a funny feeling in my belly. Lookouts have a big responsibility. Dad goes back to playing catch with my brothers while I stare at the road, waiting for a car to turn into Cooper Avenue. And sure enough, there it is! A white car.

"Car," I belt out as loud as I can. Dad winks at me and gives me a thumbs up as he and my brothers move onto the sidewalks.

I wave at the driver and so does Dad. I want more cars to drive down our street. This is fun.

Dad is teaching Robert and Eugene how to throw and catch the ball. He's also showing Eugene how to throw the perfect pitch. Some of my brothers' friends show up and join in the practice, sharing their balls and gloves. And there's Dad, playing catch with all the kids, coaching them, and paying attention to me.

Here comes another car, and it's driving much too fast. I shout "CAR" in a very loud voice, and everyone quickly jumps onto the sidewalk. My voice is strong. I am protecting my family and the neighbor's kids, too. It's an important job.

Dad winks at me. I'm his special lookout.

Before we know it, the streetlights come on and it's time to stop. Parents are in front of their houses calling for their kids to come home for dinner.

***

When I was eight years old, my brother Eugene and some of his friends were arrested for playing on the street. Playing on the street! Arrested! I was sitting in the kitchen drawing in my coloring book when Dad came in to tell us what happened. How could he be arrested for playing on the street? Was it against the law to have fun with your friends on the street?

My brother Eugene was a quiet, polite person. He always thanked Mom and Grandma for cooking lunch or dinner. Now he was a criminal for playing with his friends in the street. It didn't make sense.

Dad was furious that his son had been arrested. His face was red with anger. "Emma, where are you?" he yelled.

"I'm coming, what's wrong?' Mom screamed from the bedroom where she was sorting laundry. She ran into the kitchen in her bathrobe. Her hair was not brushed.

Speaking to Mom always calmed Dad down. He took a deep breath and said, "When Robert and I were pulling into the driveway, we saw Eugene and his friends being arrested for playing touch football in the street on Cooper Avenue."

"What? How come?" Mom asked.

"I'm going to the police precinct with Marty and some of the other fathers of the kids who were arrested," Dad said. "We'll find out what the charges are and what actually happened. I'm sure everything will be fine."

While Dad was reassuring Mom things would be fine, Robert was bringing the groceries into the house. I didn't understand what was going on, but I felt the tension, and it made me feel unwell.

"The police even grabbed the newspaper delivery boy, and he landed in the police vehicle too," Robert said.

Dad went into the bedroom. "I'll need some cash," he explained to Mom. "I may have to bail out Eugene."

✳✳✳

During the 1970s and 1980s, it was very common for the teenage boys in our safe and friendly neighborhood to play in the street on Saturday or Sunday afternoons. The younger kids in the neighborhood often sat on the curb to watch this weekend ritual and root for their favorite teams. Some of the parents sat on their front steps with their cups of coffee watching the excitement. So it wasn't surprising that Dad, Mom and our neighbors were shocked when the police arrested the kids playing ball in the street.

Grandpa Tessie and Grandpa Victor came into the kitchen just as Dad left for the police precinct. Grandma Tessie was cooking in the basement kitchen when the commotion started. She put some homemade penne on the kitchen table and set the percolator to make coffee— sustenance for the family in a difficult moment.

Mom had tears in her eyes and was repeating, "The boys always play ball on the street." Grandma Tessie knew what had happened. A certain person, a neighbor, had called the police. Grandma used a few select words in her Italian-Genovese dialect to describe this person. I didn't understand the words, but I knew from her hand motions and rapid speech that they were words I should not know or repeat in English.

Hours passed. It felt like an eternity. Daylight turned into night and Eugene was still not home. Finally, around 7:00 p.m., the side door flew open and Dad came into the room with Eugene right behind him. Mom and Grandma hugged and kissed Eugene, and then Grandma repeated those Italian words I was not supposed to hear or ever use. I still don't know what they mean.

Dad explained that all the boys would have to appear in court in front of a judge. For playing catch on the street! It didn't make sense.

A few weeks later when the boys and their fathers appeared in front of the judge, all the charges were dropped.

Mom and my grandparents were waiting anxiously in our living room. Grandpa was changing the channels on the television and Grandma was speaking rapidly and loudly in her Genovese dialect, her hands gesticulating. I was sitting on the living room floor with my Barbie dolls when Dad and Eugene came home and told us the good news. Eugene said he was hungry and Grandma got up from the sofa and went into the kitchen to make him a huge sandwich with a side of homemade potato salad.

Life on the street changed. No more softball or kickball in the street on Saturday or Sunday afternoons. The neighborhood became quiet. The voices and sounds of teenagers and children playing on Cooper Avenue died down. It was the 1980s, and electronic devices and video games were replacing play time in the street. The quiet street made a lot of people in my neighborhood very sad.

Were the boys making too much noise? Why did the parents prevent their kids from playing outside after this incident? After the charges were dismissed? Dad is not around to ask, so I have to assume he did what the other parents did: kept their kids at home and out of the street. Nobody wanted their children to be arrested again.

As I got older, my parents let me cross the street and play baseball with my friends. Dad taught me how to hold the bat with one hand while balancing on my crutches. I was a pretty good hitter, though someone else had to run the bases for me. I'm pretty sure he was standing on the front steps watching me play.

Dad in his Mets jersey

Dad's Commentary

I loved it when Dad commented on every play. Sometimes he criticized the manager for "over-managing." How could a manager "over-manage?" I wondered. Then I got it. Maybe he didn't have to change pitchers, for example. Maybe he should have left the pitcher in the game.

Dad's commentary was based on a deep knowledge of the game. He didn't read Twain, Thoreau or Hemingway; he read the baseball encyclopedia and biographies of Willie Mays, Jackie Robinson, Ted Williams and other great baseball players. Dad also understood the mechanics of the sport because he had played the game himself for so many years. He knew how to catch and throw a baseball. Sometimes he'd get up off the couch and show us how it should be done: "Put your hand without the glove over the ball to protect it from falling out of the glove," he'd say. "Many new players didn't follow this simple rule. That's why they drop the ball."

Statistics

A baseball fan has to be good in basic math to calculate baseball statistics like batting average, on base percentage, and the number of stolen bases. My dad and my older brothers taught me how to make these calculations. I remember keeping the box score for Mets games while I was still in elementary school with a good calculator and a #2 pencil. Nobody had laptops or tablets back then.

Dad and my brothers read *The New York Post* or the *New York Daily News* from back to front, starting with the sports page on the last page of the paper. After reading the write-up of the previous day's game by Phil Pepe (no relation) or Jimmy Breslin, Dad would add his own insights into the game. I listened carefully to the conversation between Dad and my brothers. If a player was on a hitting streak, Dad would joke that he hadn't changed his socks or undershirt for five days because players were superstitious. Eventually, as I learned more about the game, I would join in on the conversation.

As a young baseball fan, I enjoyed looking at the baseball cartoons in the newspapers. Bill Gallo, the *New York Daily News'* sports cartoonist, was especially creative. He could draw a player in the batter's box and capture his stance exactly.

Dad reading the newspaper on the living room couch

Superstitions

Baseball fans, like the players, are also superstitious. Picture this scene: It's Sunday afternoon and we're in the living room watching a Mets game. Dad is sitting in his recliner and I am on the floor leaning against the couch. Dad is wearing his Mets baseball cap and I am wearing my favorite Mets shirt. The Mets are winning. I don't dare budge from where I am sitting because I know if I move, the Mets will lose.

Another example: Game 6 of the 1986 National League Championship Series between the Mets and the Houston Astros. The winner would go on to play in the World Series. I was in my Astronomy class at St. John's University when the game started at 2 p.m. EST. I was listening to the game on my transistor radio, and announcing a play-by-play recap for my classmates and the professor who was also an avid Mets fan.

When class ended, Houston was up 3-0. I rushed home to watch the rest of the game, and sat on the living room floor for the next five hours until the game ended after 16 innings. The Mets won the game and advanced to the World Series. If I hadn't sat on the floor without moving while the game was still

My Mets jersey

in progress, the Mets would have lost. That's how superstitious a baseball fan can be!

The game was riveting. People were standing in the streets watching the game through the windows of television stores, or packed inside crowded bars with TV sets. The Mets brought the whole city together, a team that no one thought had a chance at playing in the World Series.

When the final out was made, there was a roar I could hear all over the neighborhood. Cars on Hylan Boulevard were honking. It seemed all the troubles of the world had been drowned out by the cheers for the home team and the love of a game called baseball.

Dad had to leave before the game was over because he worked the night shift at the post office. He listened to the rest of the game on his transistor radio, When Dad left the house, I decided to record the game so he could watch it when he got home from work. I was so superstitious that when I decided to tape the game, I genuflected and crossed my fingers that the Mets would win the game. I left the VCR tape on his recliner with a note: *Enjoy the extra innings.* Being able to watch his Mets win the National League Championship brought a lot of joy to his life.

Dad at my grandparents' 50th wedding anniversary party

Dad Meets Mom

Dad would always be the first one on the dance floor, reaching for my mom's hand to dance the Lindy or the Fox Trot and sometimes a Salsa. If Mom wasn't in the mood to dance because of her arthritis, one of my aunts or cousins would be his dancing partner.

Mom and Dad met at a dance hall in the 1950s at East 61st Street and First Avenue on the Upper East Side of Manhattan. As Mom told me, when she grew up on Roosevelt Street on the Lower East Side, young men and women would attend dances where many of them met their future husband or wife.

Dad was a very handsome man. He was taller than average at 5'11" and very slender with thick black hair, piercing eyes and great dance moves. So it's no wonder Mom fell in love with him. They got engaged in 1957 and married the next year.

Dad was then working as a school janitor in Manhattan. Four years after marrying my mother, when he was 32, he got a job as a nightshift postal clerk for the USPS. He worked in that job for 30 years.

Dad never gained much weight over the years. Until the end of his life, when he lost his appetite, he maintained his weight at 160 pounds. He walked everywhere. On Saturday mornings, he walked to the South Beach boardwalk and then back to our home which was two miles each way. All that walking contributed to his good health.

At home, Dad wore casual plaid shirts with his black ribbed eyeglasses and a Bic pen stored in his shirt pocket. He wore the eyeglasses when he read the sports section or the *Baseball Encyclopedia*. The pen came in handy when he came across the word game in the *New York Post*. He would challenge us to find as many five letter words in the highlighted word as he could find. He always won.

In 1988, Dad went into the hospital for open heart surgery. His arteries were 90 percent clogged. Stents were not an option for him. Before the operation, the nurses and doctors commented on his defined calves and strong leg muscles. After the operation, the doctor encouraged him to walk even more!

Dad was also an avid bowler who bowled until his mid-eighties when his vision became an issue. Although he could no longer bowl, he remained an enthusiastic spectator.

Mom and Dad's wedding photo

Watching Dad Shave

When I was six or seven, I began watching Dad shave. He always kept the bathroom door open so I could stand in the hallway on my crutches and watch him. I think he left the door open because he didn't want to shut me out. I could see him looking at me in the mirror. Then he'd stop shaving for a minute, turn the toilet cover down, pick me up and place me on it so I had a front row seat! It was fascinating to watch him mix the shaving cream in his Old Spice cup into a great lather that looked like whipped cream. And when he dabbed some lather on my nose and cheek, we would laugh for a few minutes until Mom suddenly appeared at the bathroom door.

What's going on in here?" she'd ask.

"I'm shaving," Dad said.

Mom just stood there for a few moments watching us, and then went back to the kitchen or to whatever else she was doing. I think that was her way of participating in the joy of these moments.

Before I learned how to walk with crutches, Dad carried me everywhere. To the store, the backyard, the beach. He was not going to let my AMC isolate me. He included me in everything, including his love for baseball. So I never felt left out or bored at home.

Dad's Old Spice shaving mug

Letting Go

I know it is not easy for a parent to let go of any child, especially a child with a disability. But my dad was able to protect me and let me go when he knew I needed to be on my own to get strong and grow, not just physically, but also mentally.

In 1972, when I was five, it was time for me to start school. When the van arrived to pick me up on the first day of school, Dad and Grandma were with me as I grabbed the railing to go down the front steps of our house, walked along the cement path that led to the metal gate, and stood there, on the sidewalk, looking at the van that would take me away from my safe home for the first time. It was a warm fall day and I was wearing shorts and a T-shirt. The bus driver greeted Dad and

Five-year-old Valerie

Grandma, and waited for me to get into the van. But I held tight onto Dad's leg. I was not going to get into that van without him.

"Dad, you have to come with me," I said.

"I can't go. I just got home from work and have to go to sleep," he said.

I began to cry and grabbed Dad's leg even harder. I didn't want to be separated.

"Valerie, you have to get on the bus," he said.

Grandma wiped away my tears.

"School is fun, Valerie," she told me.

I kept holding onto Dad's leg. I desperately wanted him to understand I absolutely couldn't leave home without him. Dad must have understood that the driver had a schedule to keep, and my antics were holding him up. So he talked to the driver, in his calm and polite manner, and the driver agreed to let Dad ride on the van with me. Problem solved. Dad came with me to school.

At school that first day, the Director of the United Cerebral Palsy (UCP) Center explained to me that my dad couldn't take me to school every day. I was nervous getting on the school bus by myself the next day, but somehow I got over it.

A Letter to My Father on My Wedding Day

On the day I married Fernando, September 7, 2024, I decided to write my dad a letter. Dad died five years before my marriage, but he was still with me, a part of my life. And I wanted him to know how happy I was.

September 7, 2024

Hi Dad,

It's a great day to get married, the weather is overcast, and the Mets are red-hot. I think they are going to make the playoffs.

I finally found the perfect mate to share my life with. Just like you and mom, the love we share is rare. You met him several times before your death in 2019; Fernando attended your 60th wedding anniversary party. Fernando is the angel that has been sent to me and mom. He cares for both of us so much.

Dad, I'm marrying a man that you would have loved and be so happy to call your son-in-law. He holds the door open for me, picks me up at the bus stop, and cares for mom as if she's his natural mother. Mom and Fernando have developed a wonderful relationship which makes me love him even more. You don't need to worry about mom because he loves her as much as he loves me.

I wish you were here to share this special day. I made sure to put the New York Mets on display at the wedding. I found a sign that says "I Love The New York Mets." It's Fernando's favorite team too; I converted him. Not to the Mets exactly, but to baseball in general. He played baseball in college but preferred track and field before he met me.

I know you aren't here to walk me down the aisle or give me away to Fernando, but I have felt your presence from the moment I arrived at Nino's Restaurant. Even though it was cloudy, as soon as we stepped out of the limo, the sun came out. I know that was you giving me you're blessing.

Of course, I would have wanted you to be here in the physical sense, but you are here in the spiritual sense. And it's a beautiful day. There's music and I can imagine you and Mom doing the Lindy Hop together.

Me and Dad at his 80th birthday party

Today is the beginning of something beautiful. I know you are watching with the baseball angels.

Miss and love you,

Valerie

The 2024 New York Mets

My Dad would be proud of the 2024 New York Mets. He would have said, "The Mets gave us a great run in getting so close to the World Series." I had those same feelings in September of 2024 when it looked like the Mets and Yankees would meet in the October classic. Mets and Yankees fans were for the first time rooting for each other's team in the hope they would meet in the World Series. As a native New Yorker and Mets fan, I knew a "Subway Series" between our two great teams would be unbelievably exciting!

During the last six weeks of the baseball season, the people of New York City seemed to be concerned only about the baseball standings and whether the Mets and the Yankees would play each other in the World Series. The last time I saw such excitement among baseball fans was in 1986 when everyone in New York City rooted for the Miracle Mets.

In 2024, I didn't watch the Mets games as often as I did in the past because of my hectic work schedule and the time it took to plan my wedding. At the All-Star game, the Mets were 10 games out of the wild-card playoff. But on the last weekend of the season, the team clinched a postseason berth by beating the highly favored Atlanta Braves 8-7 on September 30. The Mets went on to beat the Milwaukee Brewers and the Philadelphia Phillies in the playoffs before losing to the Los Angeles Dodgers in the National League Championship Series, 4-2. The Mets gave all they had but came up short.

I truly believe that during the season my Dad was sending pointers to the Mets manager and players from heaven on how to turn their season around and keep the dream alive for all of their fans, especially me.

When the Mets didn't make it to the World Series, I felt sad, but full of hope for the next season. My Dad taught me to consider what the positive outcomes of the current season mean for the team's next season "There is always a next season" he told me. That was a valuable lesson for me, the baseball fan, and for me, a disabled person, It has helped me avoid the feeling of being defeated, a feeling I've never felt!

Getting to the Stadium

I didn't go to a baseball game until 1987 when I was 20 years old. A friend of mine had box seats at Shea Stadium on the third base side. Our seats were just a few rows up from the field, so we had a closeup view of the players and the Mets dugout. On television, the dugout appeared much closer to the home plate and the baseball diamond.

The vendors were carrying tubs of hotdogs, hot pretzels, beer and cotton candy. They balanced the tall tubs of goodies on their heads in what was a truly amazing balancing act. The fans passed the money to the vendor in a chain. The vendors were dressed in the orange and blue team colors of the Mets, and on their front and back were signs showing the item and the cost of what they were selling.

The blue cotton candy wrapped in plastic in tall racks appealed to the kids. The vendors carried the cotton candy bags on long sticks nearly four feet taller above their heads. I believe they did this so the little ones sitting in the stand could easily see what they were selling and beg their parents for cotton candy.

Valerie at Citi Field in 2009

***

Dad and I never went to Shea Stadium, or to the newer stadium at Citi Field, to watch a New York Mets game. Since Dad worked the night shift and sometimes overtime on Saturdays, the only time he could spend with his family was Sunday. Being with us kids on Sunday was special for him.

Traveling to Shea Stadium from Staten Island was a long journey. Dad didn't drive, so we'd have to go to the game on public transportation. That meant taking the Staten Island Railway to the Staten Island Ferry, and then catching the train to Queens. If we made all the connections, it would take us at least two hours to make the journey.

But Dad made watching a baseball game together at home fun for all of us. And though we would have loved to eat some of that blue cotton candy sold at the stadium, Dad made sure we had either a dessert or some chocolate to enjoy.

Dad finally got the chance to attend a game at Shea Stadium with my mom in the 1960s. Mom tells me she was bored but Dad loved every minute. He didn't attend another game until the early 1990s when he went to Citi Field with my brother Robert and two nieces. Robert had arranged for them to sit in exclusive private seating where waiters served them food. This was the last time my Dad went to a game. I think he preferred watching games on television.

Baseball Stadiums in Other Cities

After my first marriage ended in divorce in 2008, I began traveling on my own. I decided to explore this great country of ours and go to places that interest me. Like baseball stadiums. To date, I've been to 19 major league and five minor league stadiums across the country. Each team has loyal and devoted fans. Just like the Mets.

My favorite ballpark is the PNC Park in Pittsburgh, home of the Pittsburgh Pirates. It opened in 2001 and is disability accessible and pedestrian friendly. It's a short walk from downtown Pittsburgh across the Roberto Clemente Bridge that's closed to traffic on game days. Walking across the bridge with Pirates' diehards was a memorable experience. When I reached my seat at the stadium, I was greeted by an older gentleman dressed in the black and gold colors of the Pittsburgh Pirates. He said, "If you need anything, my name is Tony."

I was impressed with the smooth operation of the stadium, its accessibility and security, and the friendly crowd. A woman with a disability alone in a strange city is vulnerable, but at this stadium I felt safe and comfortable.

Dad's Baseball Caps

On sunny Sunday mornings, Dad would sit in the backyard reading the newspaper and drinking a cup of Sanka coffee. He always wore a white T-shirt and blue shorts with his black rimmed eyeglasses leaning on the rim of his nose. He was never without a baseball cap protecting his receding hairline from the sun. He had a collection of baseball caps that he kept in Eugene's bedroom after Eugene got married.

Mom made my old bedroom her office where she kept her bills and the household bills. She was always very organized. Dad made Eugene's old bedroom his man cave where he surrounded himself with baseball and military memorabilia. He kept my brother's history library intact, and once in a while read one of the books. He would quiz us on what he learned from that book.

Dad's hat with the Mets' team colors

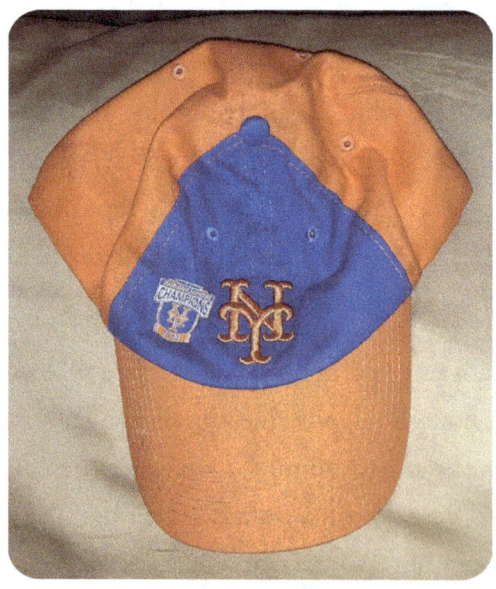

Valerie's Mets baseball hat

Baseball Gifts for Dad

I made a collage of photos and newspaper clippings for Dad of our favorite Mets players. For years it sat on Dad's dresser next to the autographed baseball I got for him at a special event at Shea Stadium—an Italian American Culture night honoring John Franco, the relief pitcher. I was at the event with a few co-workers. I told Franco that my dad was a big Mets fan and asked him to autograph the ball.

Dad had so many questions when I gave him the ball. What was it like to be on the playing field at Shea Stadium? Where did I sit? Did I meet any other players? I couldn't answer the questions fast enough for him. When I handed him the signed baseball he was as excited as a seven-year-old kid. I think Dad always dreamt about playing in a Major League ballpark, catching fly balls hit by famous baseball players, and meeting professional players.

Dad, who seldom smiled, could not stop smiling the day I gave him the baseball autographed by John Franco.

The baseball John Franco autographed for Dad

Dad, The Proud American

Every President's Day, Memorial Day, July 4th and Veteran's Day, Dad made sure the American flag hung strong and proud on our front porch. Today, more than five years since Dad passed, the flag still flies proudly on our front porch on national holidays.

I was twelve in 1979 when the American hostages were taken in Iran. The minute Dad heard the news on the television, he got a yellow ribbon from the basement and wrapped it around the evergreen on our front lawn. By the end of that week the entire neighborhood had done the same thing, on trees, telephone poles or on the gate to their property.

Dad the Postal Worker

Dad worked the night shift at the U.S. Post Office at 90 Church Street in Manhattan for thirty years. He stuck to his routine as if he was still serving as a Marine in the Korean War. He clocked in before 5 p.m. and worked until 2 a.m. He carried his brown bag lunch and postal uniform in a tote bag when he left the house to catch the 2:30 p.m. Staten Island Railway at the Old Town train station. It was a 7-minute walk to the train station and only a 5-minute train ride to the Staten Island Ferry where he caught the 3 p.m. boat. Once on the ferry, he was able to relax for approximately 22 minutes and read the afternoon version of the New York Post that he picked up at the newsstand. Dad grabbed his black-rimmed eyeglasses from the left pocket of his short-sleeved shirt and read the headlines. He also carried his transistor radio to work so he could listen to the game at lunchtime and during his break. At 2 a.m., Dad clocked out of work and walked down Church Street to catch the 2:20 a.m. ferry back home to Staten Island.

Dad sitting at our new kitchen table

I remember Mom worrying about Dad walking on the streets during the very early morning hours in the 1970s when the crime wave in New York City was at its highest point. But Dad was not afraid of the criminals. What he was afraid of were the large rats that roamed lower Manhattan. They were the size of cats. But he was never alone. He always walked to the ferry with a coworker. There was very little traffic at that time of the morning so they walked in the middle of Church Street all the way to the ferry.

Dad didn't go directly to bed when he got home. He poured himself a glass of milk and cut a slice of Holterman coffee cake that my mom had left on the counter for him. My bedroom was near the kitchen and I would hear everything even though he was very quiet. I was so glad he was home. I wouldn't get up. I just listened to the comforting sound of him in the house, cutting his cake, taking milk out of the refrigerator, and then going into the living room and turning on the television which he kept very low.

Trivial Pursuit, Books and Movies

Although Dad dropped out of school after the 10th grade, he passed the test for the General Education Degree (GED) prior to marrying my mom. He was an autodidact and an avid reader of current events, baseball, history and politics. If Dad wasn't reading the newspaper, he was reading *The Baseball Almanac*, the regular almanac, or a movie trivia book. Dad loved the movies of the 1940s and 1950s. *Casablanca* was his favorite film. He was also the King of *Trivial Pursuit*.

That made him a tough opponent when we played *Trivial Pursuit*. On snowy days when we gathered around the coffee table in the living room to play the game, Dad always came up with the correct answers to the sports, movies, history and political questions. He'd sit on the floor next to me, where I was most comfortable, and add a lot of information to his answer. If the subject was a movie, he would tell me about the background of each actor, where they were born, who they married, how many children they had, how many girlfriends, and, if the actor was an actress, if in his opinion she was attractive.

Dad playing cards with my brothers, Eugene (left) and Robert (right)

Dad would have been a great contestant on *Jeopardy*. My brother Eugene has the same skill because when we were watching the game show on television, he and Dad would both shout out the correct answers.

When Dad passed away, Mom and I went through his collection of books. The page corners of some books were turned down, as if they were earmarked for a research paper he was writing. Most of these books were in excellent condition except for one treasured book with a broken binding that Dad had tried to repair.

***

In 1976, my Dad took me and my brother Robert to the Lane Theater on Staten Island to see the movie *Rocky*. I was nine years old, old enough to go to the movies. I remember Dad made sure we got up early enough to catch the Staten Island Railway to New Dorp Lane. He wanted to get to the movie house early enough to get orchestra seats so I wouldn't have to navigate the staircase to the mezzanine level at the theater, I remember standing with them on a long ticket line.

The Lane Theater was one of the last original movie theaters on Staten Island. Sadly, it closed in 2012. I remember it vividly because I had to walk uphill on my crutches to get to the main area of the theater. This wasn't easy when I was young. The theater seemed so big, as big as the baseball stadium I had seen on television. With its plush burgundy carpet and chairs, I thought the movie theatre was an exciting place to be.

The movie screen was in front of a black curtain. The scent of buttered popcorn and the sounds of people sipping their sodas through straws made their way to my little nose and ears. The movie was going to start soon. The usher instructed everyone to find their seats, and then the lights dimmed. People were running in to grab any seat. Then the music began. I looked at Dad and sat up straight in my seat, and he did the same.

It wasn't surprising that Dad took me to see a movie about boxing. Boxing is a sport, and Dad enjoyed watching sport and wanted me to enjoy watching sport, also. He never went to a boxing match because the events were at night and tickets were expensive. If the fights were on television, he would occasionally watch them, but he watched them alone. They were too violent for a child.

Rocky is a rags to riches story about struggle and hard work. By the time the movie ended Dad was wiping tears from his eyes. The underdog had made it. I think Dad saw himself in the movie. He had strong faith, a woman that loved him, and three beautiful children. And though he didn't have a lot of money, he was rich because he was surrounded by love. Like Rocky, he'd made it.

Dad Goes to War with His Baseball Glove

When I was eight or nine years old, Aunt Theresa told me the story about the day my Dad was drafted to serve in the Korean War. We were sitting in her public housing apartment in the Bayview Houses. "Your Dad was drafted and became a Marine," she said. "He was only 20 years old."

Aunt Theresa took off her reading glasses and wiped a tear away. She told me that when the letter ordering my dad to report for service arrived, he was out with friends practicing for an upcoming baseball game with their cross-town rivals. When he got home and opened the letter from the Department of Defense, Grandma Mary and Aunt Theresa started to cry. Their boy was only 20 years old. Who would cook for him, they wanted to know?

My family in Sunset Park, Brooklyn – Grandpa Victor's first house after leaving the tenements. (Left to right) Mom and Grandma Tessie on the top step, Robert, Dad, and Eugene on the second step, and Cousin Alice standing.

I don't know how Grandpa Antonio reacted to his son being drafted. He was somewhat distant when it came to family matters, especially emotions. There are only a handful of photos of him in Dad's family photo collection. I do know he was a tailor who immigrated to America from Potenza, Italy, settled in Chicago, got divorced, and moved to the Lower East Side of Manhattan. Apparently, he worked hard and spent his spare time at the local bars rather than with his family.

I think my dad missed having a father who played catch with him.

★★★

Dad was leaving home for the first time, leaving the Lower East Side, his close-knit family, and the baseball fields he loved to play on. I think he probably was both scared and excited when he got his orders to report to boot camp in Norfolk, VA. No more hanging out late or playing baseball with his buddies, or going to the movies. Suddenly, life became extremely disciplined, much more disciplined than it was when he was living with his parents.

The base at Norfolk was segregated, which shocked him. Living on the Lower East Side, there were people of all colors and ethnic backgrounds. Color was not an issue.

Dad made friends among the Marines in his unit. Most of them were not from New York City and wanted to know what it was like to live there. They also enjoyed playing cards, and many shared Dad's love of baseball. Dad had packed his baseball glove, a baseball and a deck of cards.

★★★

While Dad was settling into his new life in Norfolk, Grandma Mary was back in the Lower East Side worrying about her son. She gathered a lot of treats, put them in a package, and mailed them to her son. The package had five packs of bubble gum, which was considered a treat back in the 1950s. The drill sergeant was not happy about Dad chewing gum. He punished Dad by commanding him to stuff his mouth with gum and sing the *Marine Corp Hymn* in front of the entire unit.

✷✷✷

When I was five or six, Dad began teaching me games I could play on the concrete pavement in the backyard. He took an empty Coca-Cola can and placed it on the ground, took a quarter out of his pocket, aimed it at the can and threw it. His first throw missed the can and landed on the concrete near the lawn chairs. So he put on his reading glasses, stood tall, and tired again. This time he gently tossed the coin in slow motion. We heard a slight 'ping' when the quarter hit the can.

Dad got very excited. "You see how easy it is? Now you try!"

I laid my right-hand crutch on the concrete and Dad placed the quarter in my tiny hand. I looked up at him. He was smiling, just the sort of encouragement I needed. I wanted to make Dad proud by hitting the can with the quarter he put into the palm of my hand.

Before I had a chance to throw the coin, Dad stood behind me, put his hand on my arm and helped me practice throwing. Dad's arm and hand were muscular and solid. After several practice attempts, I looked at Dad and said, "I'm ready!"

Dad nodded, "Ok, let's go then!"

First set of crutches

I held the quarter between my little fingers and threw it towards the Coca-Cola can, but on my first solo try, I missed.

I started to tear up and Dad immediately said, "No tears! Let's try again, remember it's only a game."

I wiped my tears with the back of my hand and looked up at Dad, and nodded.

So, there I was, balancing myself on one crutch with the precious quarter in my other free hand. I was ready. I rubbed the quarter for good luck and carefully threw it at the can.

'PING'! I hit the Coca-Cola can. Dad jumped up and lifted me into the air.

"I knew you could do it!" he shouted.

We played the game for at least an hour. I wanted to play and I wanted to win. Dad was having as much fun as I was. And when we looked up, there was Mom with a plate of grilled cheese sandwiches, glasses of milk and potato chips. She was smiling. She was happy we were having a good time, but wanted us to have lunch before we started another game.

Christmas Eve at the Pepe House

The preparation for Christmas Eve always began weeks before December 24th. Dad and Grandpa Victor would decorate the front yard and staircase leading to the front door with an array of colored lights. Dad's decorations, which he assembled in the basement, were magical. He wrapped the tiny Christmas lights around the existing poles and pipes above the large dining room table where everyone gathered. He also wrapped garland around the poles and pipes in the basement that added extra sparkle to the room.

In 2000, when Aunt Teresa moved to Staten Island from the Bayview Housing Development in Canarsie, Brooklyn, we added her Santa Claus pictures and bells with silver and red tinsel to the holiday decorations. Aunt Theresa's son, Anthony, her only child, died in a drowning accident at Riis Park in the Rockaways in 1984.

Dad kept all the Christmas decorations in the basement closet. He had all the festive colors of Christmas organized in boxes.

Even as an adult, I still feel the joy of these occasions. The memory of sitting on the basement steps in my pajamas, looking at the light glistening against the garland and tinsel, is powerful. Dad is always present. I see him placing the vases with evergreen bases in the middle of the large table. And I see all of my family—my brothers, aunt, mom and grandma—sitting around the table.

Sundays with Fernando and the Mets

No matter what I'm doing on Sunday, the Mets game is on the television or radio. Sometimes, my husband Fernando watches the game with me. I am teaching him about baseball statistics, the rules of the game, and the different strategies and plays of the game. Just like my dad taught me. Sometimes, my comments and criticisms sound just like my dad speaking.

Fernando watched baseball before he married me, but now he knows a lot more about the game and how it's played, thanks to me and my dad. Sometimes he watches a Mets game when I'm not home.

It's 2025, and my dad has been gone for over 5 years. But I believe he's managing from heaven.

Acknowledgements

I wrote this book to celebrate my relationship with my dad and our shared love of baseball and the Mets. It's with deep love that I thank him for teaching me a game that brings so many families together.

With gratitude to my mother, Emma Pepe, for her support and guidance throughout my life, and for filling in the gaps in my knowledge of my father's lifelong love of baseball and how they met and married.

To my husband, Fernando Quintero, I thank him for his enduring support, love and fortitude, and for supporting all my endeavors, especially the writing of this book. There's no other person with whom I can imagine sharing my life.

Without the support of my extended family, this story of me and my dad would not be complete.

I also wish to thank all of the people in my life who have always been there for me: Frank Baratta, Manny Blandina, Catherine Bondar, Grace Buzzetta, Felicia Chapman-Jenkins, Maria Lisa Cuzzo, Eunjoo Lee, Nancy Falcone, Vincenza Gallassio, Michele Faljean, Nancy Cicciarello-Matamoros, Brauilo Mamtoros, Melsissa Melfi, Anne Rielly, Ed Roslak, Bill Russo, Dean Santa, Paula Tramontano, Laura Van-Cott, Kenneth Van-Cott, Deb Wilborn and my colleagues at the New York City Housing Authority where I have been employed for 32 years.

Thank you to the entire AMC community here in the United States and around the world. Their positive thoughts and words gave me the energy to write another book.

My sincere gratitude to Assemblywoman Nicole Malliotakis and her staff for promoting awareness and understanding of the rare condition of Arthrogryposis Multiplex Congenita (AMC).

To my writing coach, Carol Bergman, and editor and publisher, Jim Bergman, I want to thank both of them for their support and guidance through the process of writing this book. Thanks for taking this wonderful ride with me and my dad.

Finally, I must also thank all the doctors who played an important part in my development as an independent woman despite my physical disability. They are:

Dr. Michael Donato

Dr. Louis Defeo

Giana Giordano, PA

Dr. Stephen Kulick

Dr. John Reilly

Nino Sarvida, Physical Therapist

Dr. Joseph Suarez

Dr. Harold Van Bosse

www.ingramcontent.com/pod-product-compliance
Lightning Source LLC
LaVergne TN
LVHW020415070526
838199LV00054B/3618